THE BOARDS' YEAR.

THE STORY OF MILLIONS OF STUDENTS.

HARSH ADITYA

XpressPublishing
An imprint of Notion Press

No.8, 3rd Cross Street,CIT Colony,
Mylapore, Chennai, Tamil Nadu-600004

ISBN 978-1-64951-457-8

To all my friends of class 11.

Contents

Preface

Poems and articles are part of everyone's life. Everyone does not compose poetry or write article but they do feel it. The poem is not always written for entertainment or joy, sometimes it is written to express what one feels within. Many a time some poems and article are written out of joy and also some comes during the time of sorrow. As the day is never the same for many, in the same way, the feel of the poem and article is not the same as you read it.

Well, this is not a poem in particular but a short novel like book. This has so many facts and information for the 11[th]standard student that will not let them fall into the wrong side of the long road. It will guide most of the readers for their better future and will help them to do better in every exam that they take in life.

My journey as a writer began when I aged 13 years. Though I am not professional in it, yet I appreciate my work more. We, humans, live in a world where reality is valued more than what you have done in your past. In this world, if you can write something well and appreciable then you are good at your field. I, as a writer, have many thoughts in my mind and it is not easy to pen them down forming coherence. Yet I try my best to make it attractive and sensible for the readers so that they understand and co-relate their lives if they could.

This book has a normal writing genre as it is written by a normal writer. It contains the journey of a student who gets into the first intermediate class. I am the bearer of each and every circumstance which I have composed in the form of a novel like book.

I also owe my special thanks to my school where I learned to write English Poems and also the appropriate usage of words and punctuation in sentences.

My alma matter "St.Xavier's School Sahibganj". The place where I learned the value of English. The daily speeches made me this worthy. Also to my English teacher "Mrs. Dorothy Vatsa"; who framed my English so well that today I am capable of writing a book.

I thank all my readers for having read my previous book. My motivation to keep on writing something comes from all the real-life examples which I have experienced till date.

At this age of 17 and being the student of class 12, I am writing *"The Boards' Year"*. This is a matter of great privilege and also a proud moment for me.

Acknowledgements

And yes, my lovely parents who gave me birth so that I could complete "The Bords' Year".

Oler

I acknowledge my family members, brothers, and sisters and most importantly, my most respectful senior; Jagjeet Raj.

Thank you everyone for the support.

Oler

How can I forget Sunny Kumar and Mayank Kumar Singh for making my boards' year fun at Delhi Public School, Bokaro Steel City.

Prologue

Once you read this novel, you will find your journey doubly planned and also 100% sure.

ONE
A NEW YEAR.

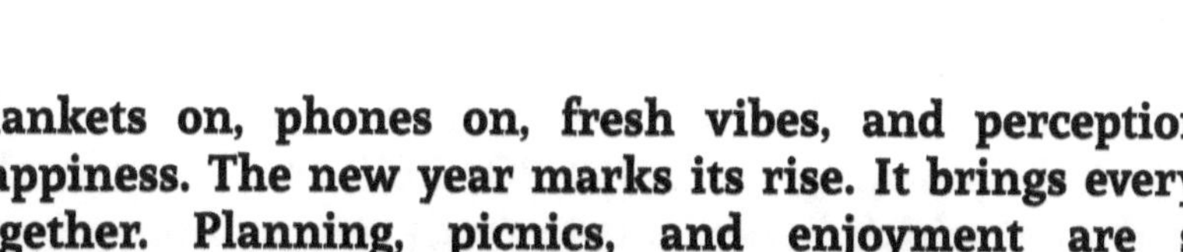

Blankets on, phones on, fresh vibes, and perception of happiness. The new year marks its rise. It brings everyone together. Planning, picnics, and enjoyment are soon implemented within few hours of its birth. The air is soon filled with the aroma of delicious food, the noise of automobiles, and the cries of the children also fill the air with excitement. The parks, resorts, restaurants, and picnic spots contain a huge crowd of people who enjoy the first day of the year with all sorts of energy in them. They celebrate the day with happiness and joy.

The New Year is not about a day, rather it is about the complete 365 or 366 days.

Well, every new year brings lots of stress in a student's life. Every year two batches of students belonging to classes 10 and 12 have to sit for their 1 month long, boards examination which begins in the month of February and ends by the end of March. This fear of boards makes a student more cautious in their studies and makes them score well. As the day approaches, the fear increases. Many students' PRE-BOARDS also occur during the month of January. Those students are more bothered about their PRE's.

The first stroke a student gets is when the date-sheet of the board examination gets released. The rush here begins. A student starts to make his time-table, sets the alarm at 4 o'clock in the morning, sticks the BOARD'S date-sheet on the walls against which he/she sits to study. The sample papers are bought and solved weekly, self mock tests begin, prayers to God are chanted daily, essay and letter writing practice daily, completion of 10 chapters of Mathematics daily, and much more preparation ways are adopted by a student.

Pupils' workloads increase day by day. Their stress and tensions start to overpower their happiness and joy. The student suffers maximum during this period. They are surrounded by society's pressure, boards' pressure, school's pressure, and also family pressure. It's totally on the student how does he/she handles it. The person to tackle all these pressures calmly by laboring daily finds himself/herself in the place where he/she has dreamt to be. It's not that the ones who are incapable of handling the pressure are not happy, they may be happy only if they agree that whatever they received was only because they strived for it.

ᗡᗡᗡ

The Month of preparation is not entirely based on books and pens, it's the one and half months' leave for the preparation and everyone does not sit with books for the entire 24 hours. Students need a break to make themselves feel the existence of a world outside books. No one cand be so much engrossed in books for the whole day. A student takes a day's break only if he is confident in all the subjects that are to be asked in their respective examinations. A break may include anything positive like playing with friends, taking some fresh air, sun-basking, walking in the early morning, clicking photos, to wander around with friends or family.

▷▷▷

During the preparation period, a student's mind is filled with negativity. He/She starts to think about the consequences if he/she is unable to bring good grades in the examination. He/She starts to lack confidence in him/her. The negativity begins to overpower positivity. This is the common case that comes into the minds of the toppers also. The only tip to tackle it is to be constant and regular in one's work until the examinations get terminated.

TWO
THE BOARDS.

With the warm weather and cold winds hitting the cheeks of the candidates; standing in the assembly and eagerly waiting to take their first exam. The waiting period soon ends and the pupil marks themselves into the examination hall. With anxiety in mind and body, the student sits for the first exam. With two to three hours of a continuous fight between the mind and questions, the pupil comes out with joy as he/she has tackled the first paper well.

The same process continues for all the papers. The study-leave allotted for certain subjects makes a student more confident in his preparation. It is during this time that one does not care about his/her results. He/She puts a continuous effort in his/her work and tries to make all his exams end in a joyous way.

A month-long examination tiers all the students, be it for the class 10thers or 12thers.

Having finished half of the examination, a student starts to lose the pressure that he /she had on the day the boards had begun. The pressure and efforts decreased the workloads and got transferred into the ink on the exam sheet.

ᐅᐅᐅ

A human's mind is never still, it always has something in it which either disturbs the person's mind only or it disturbs the whole community. As soon as the examinations approach its end, the student's mind is now diverted towards the various kinds of excitement that he/she would be doing after the completion of the boards. The student soon who started his/her examination with a blast has now moved towards ending his/her examination anyhow. The same student who didn't waste his/her study-leave for even an hour has now started to waste two to three vital hours of a day in dreaming about the activities to be done by him/her after the completion of the examination, rather than using those crucial time in studying.

The most vital situation to be taken care of, here comes. The part that a student has to play from getting away all these thoughts is to only concentrate and focus on his/her work which is important for that particular instant. Someone who controls his/her mind right from the beginning of the examination has a higher possibility to do well.

ᐅᐅᐅ

Slowly and steadily, the time runs and the students; who have engrossed themselves so much into their books are even not aware of it. They remember the last date and subject.

The 10thers and 12thers sit for the final time in the same examination hall where they have been evacuating the ink from the pen for the past one month. The students' mind has two feelings, one is to give the best for the one last time and terminate the season of exam happily and the other feeling is to enjoy and only enjoy after the completion of a long period of exams.

▷▷▷

The reason for a tornado in many students' life finally comes to an end by the end of March and frees the boys and girls from the headache of following a constant, long and arranged time-table for more than a month.

THREE
SATISFACTION.

The nights now begin at 5 o'clock in the morning and mornings begin at 11 o'clock for those same people who used to get up at 5 o'clock and went to bed at 12 o'clock. The time-table suddenly changes, the phones are on, bats and ball in boys' hands, and the air which once contained stress is now filled with happiness, joy, and excitement. The environment experienced an abrupt change with the change of seasons.

The satisfied pupil enjoys their vacation. An average student wants to do all the things in a limited span of time. He/She wants to extract their hidden talents and use them in the best way they could. Few of them succeed in doing so and inculcate an interest in it. Well, it is very important also. The reason being, today only study is not valued, all sorts of creativity which can benefit the nation and is of great value is more valued and also appreciated everywhere.

The vacation after boards is really very useful for most of the students. The pupils use their time in many activities, for example, someone practices his/her sport which they missed during the boards, someone reads interesting books, magazines, and fictitious novels, some also prefer to watch movies full of excitement, adventure, and fiction, some enjoy their time in roaming around the country, some students explore their own town in the best way they could, some ride bikes and move about here and there all the day, some sit and think about their career and plan their future and there are also a bunch of students who use this free time in studying something which will be useful to them in the next year.

The Underages start to get their personal phones, laptops, computers, and other luxury items. These items play a crucial role in turning a student's life. It either destroys someone's life or makes someone's life. It has both disadvantages and advantages. The students now start considering themselves as mature and they think themselves superior which starts to deteriorate the student's performance in everything. He/She also faces many consequences during this vacation where he/she has no alternative, he/she has to suffer because of this nature.

FOUR

A THOUGHTFUL HEAD.

Soon, the vacation also subsides and another month begins. The month of April. Having nurtured all the talents and hobbies, the student has another mission in life, he/she has to go to the second innings of life. He/She has to apply for the higher studies which is very difficult as compared to the preliminary classes.

The time to apply for classes 11 and 12 has come. A normal student starts to search for good schools across the country which is also near to his/her town. He/She begins to enquire about the schools selected by them, they try to search the vacancies, criteria for admission, minimum percentage required to get into the school, and also the entrance examination which will lead one to get into it. The dates to fill the forms are taken out, the forms are filled, the student now prepares for that final test which will take one into their dream school. He/She prepares hard to crack the test, they sit for the test and after two hours of the test, they return with different faces. Someone very happy, few sad, a few without any reaction. The result is generally out by the end of the very day and the moment when a student types his/her enrollment number to check whether he has qualified for the test or not is the worst feeling ever.

ᑭᑭᑭ

There are two possible chances:

1.

   The Result turns out to be positive.

2.

   The Result turns out to be negative.

Based on the first point a student has to fulfill the minimum percentage criteria to get admitted into his/her school of dreams.

The second point makes one very sad, disheartened, anxious and weak. If a student fails to crack the entrance examination of a particular school, he/she must first not be disheartened. He/She must try to apply in another school of his choice and must prepare for the second one. He/She should never give up, they should keep on trying until they find their choice.

Getting admitted to any school is good, no school in the country is bad. Each institution has its own value. The students who unfortunately could not enter into the schools of their choice must get into a school which also has some name and he/she must try to give his/her best there and perform excellently in academics because what matters in the end, is the result that you bring and not the school from where you bring.

ᑭᑭᑭ

___One must always aim for a long term fame and not short-termed fame.___

Oler

Does everyone join the school after their matriculation?

The answer to this is NO. The competition begins after class 10th. A student who aspires to be an engineer or doctor goes to a separate line. He/She joins a coaching institute in order to crack JEE and NEET to qualify for an engineer or doctor respectively. Student migrates from a place to another depending upon their ambitions and also convenience.

It's not that, a person who wishes to be an engineer jo has to crack JEE only. The reason why 9lakhs students apply for this entrance exam is that, by cracking this JEE, one gets himself/ herself into the best technical institutes of India. The other reason is IITs are cheap when compared to good private engineering colleges, the other reason being, the awesome faculty and best placements are given to a student every year.

The same reason is also applicable for the candidates who crack NEET. NEET allows one to admit himself/herself into the best government colleges of India in order to get the best knowledge from their esteemed faculty members.

For those, who find JEE and NEET as new terms:

1.

   JEE stands for Joint Entrance Exam which is organized by NTA(National Testing Agency) every year. This

examination is valid for the students who have PCM(Physics, Chemistry, and Maths) as their base subjects in classes 11 and 12. It takes place in two stages. The first stage is JEE Mains which takes place twice a year in the months of January and April. One who qualifies this exam enters into the second stage called JEE Advanced which takes place in the month of May. The syllabus is based on CBSE and only class 12th students can appear for this exam. After qualifying JEE Advanced, if one's rank is under 10000 then he/she gets into the IITs and the others may get some other government colleges depending upon their ranks. The engineering colleges train the undergraduates for B.Tech and M.Tech degrees.

2.

NEET stands for National Eligibility cum Entrance Test. It is also organized by NTA every year in the months of May. Students who have PCB(Physics, Chemistry, and Biology) as their base subjects in classes 11 and 12 can appear for this exam. It leads to the best medical colleges in India. It is conducted in only one stage. The selection here is also on the basis of rank and marks that you obtain out of 720. The medical colleges train the undergraduates for the MBBS and BDS degrees.

Well, one can also prepare for this exam while schooling. The line means that if a student aspires to get into IITs as well as he/she wants to do schooling then he/she is also welcomed to do it. One can join the coaching institutes in a place where his school lies and begin his/her preparation. The students who rank under 100 start their preparation from class 9th onwards.

Not everyone joins coaching institutes just after the boards get terminated. Most of the students join after the boards' result.

• 13 •

FIVE

HARD WORK PAYS OFF.

After the completion of boards, one spends his/her time in many ways. Many students leave for their new journey, some of them qualify the entrance test of the reputed schools and wait for their boards' result, a few still do not bother about anything and loiter around in the city. The month of April and May decides what a student will be doing in the future.

April passes, May enters. As soon as the month changes to may, everyone starts to inculcate the same stress and tension which was taken by the students during the boards. The students count the number of days left for the result to be declared. This month, the stress and pressure are not only on the students but also on the parents and family members.

Finally, the date arrives for which so much of labor was done. Right from the beginning of the day, the students, their family members, and the school are in a situation that can not be explained. The time allotted for the result to be out approaches with the tik of the clock. The adrenaline secretion increases, pressure increases, heartbeats increases, and the body starts to become warm.

The moment has come when one has to type his/her roll number on the required space. This moment is of course not the best moment for many students. Soon by the end of the day, everyone has known their results. The toppers wait for the other day to see their names in the local newspaper. The student who finds himself/herself in the newspaper is proud, his/her family is proud and his/her school is proud.

There are also some students who do not score very good marks. A small tip for them is that they get only that much for which they strive. They received what they deserved. They must always accept the reality and always try to do some good and work harder than what they did the previous day. Accepting reality is also not an easy task, a few take a very short time to do it and some take a long time. Moving on is also a very important key. One must always move on from their past to create a better future.

SIX

THE BEGINNING OF A NEW JOURNEY.

Having received the results of boards, the students now gain confidence in achieving big in their life. With this new potential, he/she moves ahead in life and climbs the second step. The step which will decide their future. From here begins the journey of class 11th and 12th. Life takes a turn from this very stage. The easier things start to seem tougher, the possible dreams start to seem impossible and the luxurious future starts to shatter in front of the eyes.

It becomes very difficult for a person to study and concentrate in an entirely new place. He/She misses his/her home. The change is seen in many things like food becomes tasteless, sleep becomes more addictive, study is neglected and calls serve as the only source to exist.

ᐁᐁᐁ

Well, on attending the first class of a coaching institute or of a school, the first thing that a teacher tells is to forget all the teachings of class 10th. To forget a years' teaching is very very difficult. The other difficulties also come up eventually. The difficulties in concentrating, getting up early in the morning, going to bed early, maintaining a proper time-table for the next two years, and to go to the school or coaching regularly.

Before coming to the desired place or to start one's 11th and 12th a person should prepare to live in the city and get habituated to it. Secondly, he/she must make a time-table which he/she has to follow regularly, Thirdly, he/she should only sit for study when he finds all his works to be completed or else it would act as a distraction which would make him/her lose concentration.

ᐅᐅᐅ

This beginning marks the biggest change in students' life. He/She tackles all the possible difficulties and marches towards his/her future. All that a student suffers in this stage is mainly because of the following reasons.

1.

To make his/her life comfortable in the future. As the results of class 12th will get one into the best colleges of India and the preparation to crack different competitive exams in the field of science include the entire syllabus of class 11th and 12th.

2.

To make his/her parents, family proud of them by obtaining excellent grades.

3.

To let their parents' money not go into waste. Higher studies are expensive. Parents have to pay a huge sum of money to let their son/daughter study. So one must never think of wasting his/her parents' money. He/She must do

the work for which he/she has been sent to the new places.

One who does not waste the even single second of his 11th and 12th is sure to succeed in his/her near future.

SEVEN
MANAGEMENT AND STABILITY.

A students' first month during this phase is the toughest month of his life. He/She has to manage his time and get the best use of it. One experiences the value of time after getting into their 11th and 12th. The 24hours which we didn't value in our childhood is now highly valued and understood. One starts understanding that there are only 24hours in a day and there are a hell lot many things to be done regularly. The mind is full of managing things in a proper way and doing it in the best way.

A students' first priority is their books. One's time with books shows his/her laboring hours. Pupils who are in the coaching institutes have to study only of the coaching regularly, they have to work on their questions regularly, clearing doubts and doing a question in an easier way. They get 24hours of time in a day to do all their works. There is another group of students who has to concentrate on their boards right from the time they enter into class 11th. They focus on subjective approaches to the questions, clearing their doubts and making the boards easy for them. Some students also focus on reading multiple books for concepts and questions. These groups of students also get only 24hours of time in a day. There is another group of students who has to focus on competitive exams as well as their boards simultaneously. These students have more pressure when compared to the pressure of the students in the coaching institutes or the students who do only schooling.

The pressure on the students is also of the schools' internal examinations. They have to strive for obtaining good scores in the internal exams as well as attend the institutes to which they go. It is not very easy to do both things on the same day. The amount of time to be dedicated to the schools' examination must be more during the exam time.

⊳⊳⊳

All that matters here is how a student manages his time to touch all the subjects thoroughly. He/she has to give equal priority to all the subjects that they have chosen for their studies. The scheduled timetable must be maintained and followed consistently. To maintain stability between studies and other activities, one must always give most of his free time to the activities in which he/she is keenly interested. Doing the activities almost every day for even a small duration of time makes one confident in it and he/she can stay fit physically as well as mentally.

Management and stability are the most important and the only rule to succeed in class 11 and 12. See, all the time you can't just sit with books and expect of coming up with good marks or ranks. Your case study for that particular exam must be foolproof.

⊳⊳⊳

What is the basic thing that you can do when you are simply doing nothing, *viz* during your preparing hours when you find that you have done your part for that particular day; when you feel that you have solved sums, studied for the required time that you have decided to do and also done the activities at least for the limited amount of time. During those free periods, what you can do is just go through some of the previous years' question papers of the entrance examination which you are going to appear for. During this process, one can see all the variations of the question, change in the pattern of setting the questions in the examination and the most important part is that one can understand the total number of questions that can be asked from a particular chapter.

The importance of a case study is that it'll give one the way to prepare themselves in a proper and correct manner. It will also create an impression on the student's mind that he/she has to study a particular portion of the subject thoroughly and consistently.

Such pressure on the student goes until the first vacation given by their schools/coachings. Students of class 11 all across the country get their first vacation in the month of October; the Diwali vacation.

EIGHT

A Short Vacation.

EVERYONE IS BACK HOME.

Oler

So, the warrior returns back to the place where everything began. The first request that is made to the parents by them is that they want to eat everything made at their home. The students are back to their comfort zones and they switch on the mode of enjoyment and begin it right from the time when they stepped in their yard.

What do they miss the most is their old school. They want to meet their friends, teachers, and all the people whom they left while going away. It is always their wish to meet and have fun with them. The school buildings bring their nostalgia and these young chaps get carried away by all those mischiefs that were done by the once they were at the school. Even the teachers feel so good to meet their old students.

Happiness and glory began all the way from here.

Generally, the students get back to their yards during the 10 days of Diwali vacation. These 10 days of leave turns out to be the best days of their life. Every person waits for this 10 days leave. Diwali is the festival of lights. It brings light in the life of every student, it makes everyone forget all their problems and gives them a boost to enjoy this time with their family. The tension to aim at rank 1 is out of the mind for few days. The only advice to enjoy this peak time is to forget about studies and DPPs. One's focus must be on family, cricket grounds, soulful destinations and the best view of the city.

NINE
NOSTALGIA DOMINATES PRESENT.

Everyone is back to normal. The same routine continues and the noise of the students fills the entire classroom. The benches and desks again witness the cheerful and enthusiastic screams of the students. The competition is all set to knock again. This time the journey is going to be long. Every single person has their own motivation to crack the examination. Having boosted up from their home town, the warriors have now returned to their arena to fight and mark their name registered in history.

Earlier, I mentioned, "Every single person has their own motivation." This line has a huge impact on everyone. The Diwali vacation mad the students happy as well as cheerful. These people started to think and reason out plenty of things during the vacation. The time when they are back in the classroom, they remember all the happy moments cherished by them. Their eyes are full of tears and their cheeks turn red. The love and affection of their parents are now being missed by these little chaps. People do want to go out and hang out, explore new places; but once they settle in an entirely new place, it does not become easy for them to persist. They might wander around the place but they never appreciate their life.

In the end, they end up saying," I want to be back home."

❧❧❧

Just like them, every school/coaching going student has the same feeling. Nobody is actually happy with their life. Can anybody change the way things go on? No. We will have to learn to live and survive in what we have. If we learn this fact of life, there is nothing that will hurt us. Everything will seem to be joyful and will be celebrated with so much fun.

TEN
THE EXAM'S PRESSURE.

The peak time when everyone is busy witht their best companion is the examination time. Every student at this time has their books in their hand. They put in efforts altogether. Thinking about no affairs and nothing they just read the texts and tries to complete all those stuff which they had studied the whole year. This work is definitely not easy.

Every teacher asks us to read the chapters daily so that we may not hurry during the exams. To be very honest, I am also a student and I have tried this advice when I was in my 10th standard, I read my lessons regularly but when I felt my exams at the door, I had to revise my syllabus. What I felt during this activity was that, when I began to revise my lessons, it became very easy for me to go through. The tough chapters were learned in a very quick time. I didn't struggle much in doing so. The teachers are not fools that they repeat something every time. Everything that they speak makes sense.

There is so much burden on the students to clear their examinations. They think of the parents' expectations with them which makes them think in two ways.

1.

What would happen if I fail?

2.

I would join the best college if I score well.

Usually, the first thought hits every student. They start fearing their examinations, which makes them distracted from their studies and ultimately they do not score well. The famous *"Shrimad Bhagwad Gita"*asks us not to think about the results. It also preaches us to concentrate on our work and do it wisely. Our works will decide our place in the future. Till then we only have to keep trying as much as we could.

I would suggest everyone to never think too much about the second thought. It definitely adds positivity to our life but in the same way, it even harms us. As, if we keep on thinking about our future we may lose time to concentrate on our examinations and it will surely harm us in one or the other way.

ϼϼϼ

Concentrating on the present is the only and perfect solution to work and make our works better.

ELEVEN
RESULTS.

Everyone who stepped out of their city for the first time in search of knowledge and good competition has now reached that point of time when everything is going to be revealed. The only news that flashes all along the tv screens is about the results. Even the student faces a mixture of feelings. They begin to get confused about all the different scopes in life. Many of them even try to reason out so many things that are completely irrelevant.

The parents and family members are eager to know the result of their child. Normally, everyone wishes the best result for their children and also prays for their good future. The dates are out for the declaration of the results. This makes everyone curious about their future. The students start to recall all their efforts that they had invested to clear the examination. Those of the students who hadn't finished their exams properly are more tensed and start to fear. This is the normal fact that everyone experiences in their life. Even after giving the best out of something, we humans have the nature to think and pressurize ourselves for having done that work more sincerely and perfectly. We are rarely happy with what we do.

Everyone has their results now. Like the two sides of a coin aren't the same, in the same way, every student is not happy with what they have received.

ᗡᗡᗡ

Results are not always positive. It is not that results always bring happiness to a family. It always brings happiness to their faces who had strived really hard. People sometimes forget their worth and take a drastic step to end their life after failing to achieve something.

We can not let our emotions win over our present. It is a fact that we never had the decision to get this beautiful life, so we should also never think of ending it because we have no right to do so. We have our parents and also the family so why don't we think of them before leading our mind towards such ideas. Taking our life will neither improve the decided results nor it will change the truth into false. The basic and best solution to failure is to accept reality and move further with whatever we contain.

This is for all the youngsters out there, you have been the best creation of the Almighty, what happens if it didn't get cleared in the first attempt? Even Thomas Alva Edison didn't make the electric bulb in the first attempt. Just wait for the time and till then be focussed and self-centered. You will shine brighter than everyone.

Advices.

So here I bring up the most important part of this short novel. The basic idea of achieving something great. What we want to do is the only motive behind all our hard works and struggles. We have been doing many things till now with entire labor and potential. What do we expect in the end? A taste of happiness and also a success. Everyone doesn't land in the same arena, there are people who end up being a common man with no success in life. They criticize themselves everyday for not laboring hard at that time when they were supposed to do. They repent for not getting the golden days back.

I don't know what success means individually.
In my view, success is that part of life when we are happy for everything, and most importantly, we never repent for anything that has already happened in the past.

ppp

Along with success come enemies. The vital and real-world has so many deep secrets. It cannot digest the happy days of a person. It has to do something so unreal that will make a person guilty even for a very minute mistake. When you have bad luck, even a small countless mistake can make you lose your life.

Be what you have always wanted yourself to be. The world is neither gonna feed you nor appreciate you on your success. Its' fakeness is so drastic that even the trustees turn out to be your enemies.
You have to hold yourself; only for your dignity and self-

respect. The money you earn in the future will surely decide the way of your life but it will never decide your character. Your character will only be known by your personality.

You will find people during the different phases of life. Everyone's presence in this fake world will matter, even if that person entered into your life for only a second. The time that they spend in your life doesn't matter, all that does is the impact which they lay in your life during their presence. In the end, they will depart and teach you some of the best lessons which you will always keep alive in your mind. People will sign so many treaties, pacts, and petition but you never know what they would do just the next moment. Only 1 in lacks of fake people will stay with you. Even that doesn't happen with everyone.
Excluding all the unnecessary people from your life, you will always find two-person always at your back. They will be your parents forever. Even after their demises, they will remain with you all the time.

ꙮꙮꙮ

"The time to rule your life only begins when you dethrone evil out of your kingdom."